W9-ABY-401

Jones Library, Inc.
43 Amity Street
Amherst, MA 01002

WITHDRAWN

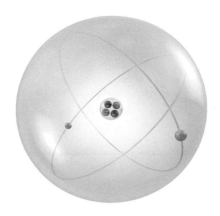

⊙Discovery
EDUCATION™

Published in 2014 by The Rosen Publishing Group, Inc.
29 East 21st Street, New York, NY 10010

Copyright © 2014 Weldon Owen Pty Ltd. Originally published in 2011 by Discovery Communications, LLC

Original copyright © 2011 Discovery Communications, LLC. Discovery Education™ and the Discovery Education logo are trademarks of Discovery Communications, LLC, used under license. All rights reserved.

All rights reserved. No part of this book may be reproduced in any form without permission in writing from the publisher, except by a reviewer.

Photo Credits: **KEY** tl=top left; tc=top center; tr=top right; cl=center left; c=center; cr=center right; bl=bottom left; bc=bottom center; br=bottom right; bg=background

CBT = Corbis; CERN = CERN; DT = Dreamstime; IQ = Image Quest; iS = istockphoto.com; N = NASA; SH = Shutterstock; TF = Topfoto; TPL = photolibrary.com; wiki = Wikipedia

front cover iS; **6–7**bc, tc SH; **7**br iS; tr, tr SH; **8**bc DT; bl iS; **8–9**bc iS; **10**cr N; br, tl, tr SH; **11**cl iS; bl SH; **13**tl CBT; **14**br, cr iS; bl SH; cl TF; **15**bc, bl, br, cr, tl, tr, tr IQ; **16**bl, br, cl, tl iS; **18**bl, cl TF; **19**br TF; **21**tl, tl SH; **22**bc TF; br TPL; **23**tc iS; bc wiki; **24**bl, cl CERN; **24–25**tc CERN; **25**tl, tr CERN; **26**cl, cr, tl TF; **27**c, cl, tl, tr TF; cr wiki; **28**cl N; **29**bc, c N; **30–31**bg iS; **32**bg wiki

All illustrations copyright Weldon Owen Pty Ltd. **6**bl, **9**tc, **17**b Peter Bull Art Studio; **25**c, **28**br Andrew Davies/Creative Communications; **12**bc Lionel Portier; **18–19**, **22**tr Godd.com

Weldon Owen Pty Ltd
Managing Director: Kay Scarlett
Creative Director: Sue Burk
Publisher: Helen Bateman
Senior Vice President, International Sales: Stuart Laurence
Vice President Sales North America: Ellen Towell
Administration Manager, International Sales: Kristine Ravn

Library of Congress Cataloging-in-Publication Data

Stephens, David, 1945– author.
 A material world : what is matter? / by David Stephens.
    pages cm. — (Discovery education. How it works)
 Includes index.
 ISBN 978-1-4777-6325-4 (library) — ISBN 978-1-4777-6326-1 (pbk.) — ISBN 978-1-4777-6327-8 (6-pack)
 1. Matter—Properties—Juvenile literature. 2. Matter—Constitution—Juvenile literature. I. Title.
 QC173.16.S73 2014
 530.4—dc23
                        2013023583

Manufactured in the United States of America

CPSIA Compliance Information: Batch #W14PK2: For Further Information contact Rosen Publishing, New York, New York at 1-800-237-9932

A MATERIAL WORLD
WHAT IS MATTER?

DAVID STEPHENS

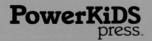

PowerKiDS press.

New York

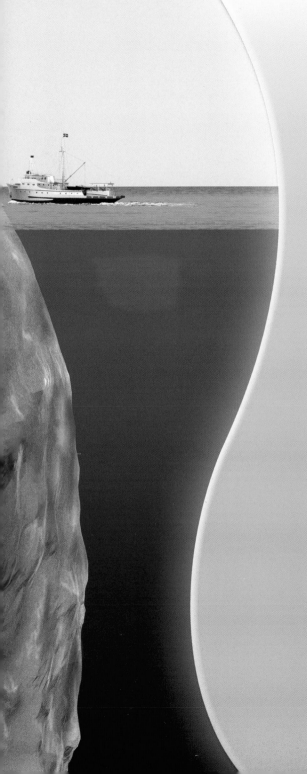

Contents

What Is Our World Made Of?................6

What Is Matter?....................8

States of Water....................10

A Closer Look 12

Changing Matter 14

Wacky, Weird, and Wonderful 16

Splitting the Atom....................18

The Big Bang 20

Matter and Antimatter....................22

Particle Accelerators 24

Famous Scientists....................26

Unsolved Mysteries....................28

Glossary....................30

Index 32

Websites....................32

What Is Our World Made Of?

Air
Air is everywhere and always on the move. Fire will not burn without air.

For the past 3,000 years, humans have wondered about the makeup of the universe. In about 440 BC, Empedocles, a Greek philosopher, proposed that everything was made from four elements: water, earth, fire, and air. He got the idea from observing wood burning on a fire. He saw water given off as steam. He felt air coming from the fire. He noticed the ashes were like the earth. He concluded that fire changed everything into the basic elements. The idea that the universe was made from four elements spread around the world. Hindus and Buddhists added a fifth element—ether, the space around us. The Chinese had their own theory based on the elements of wood, fire, earth, metal, and water. These five elements are used to this day in Chinese medicine.

Today's scientists still explore this question, and they now have a name for everything in the universe. It is called matter.

Five elements of Ayurveda
This ancient Indian healing practice believes everything in the universe is made from five building blocks or elements: earth, water, fire, air, and ether.

The ancient Greek scholar Democritus called the smallest piece of matter atomos, *meaning "indivisible."*

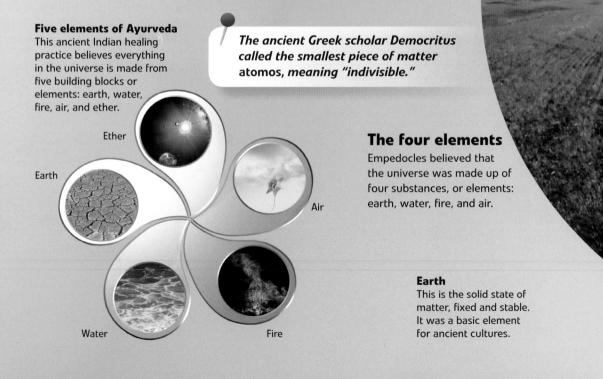

Ether

Earth

Air

Water

Fire

The four elements
Empedocles believed that the universe was made up of four substances, or elements: earth, water, fire, and air.

Earth
This is the solid state of matter, fixed and stable. It was a basic element for ancient cultures.

Fire
Fire (heat or energy) has the power to change things from solids to liquids and gases.

Burning logs
These were Empedocles' inspiration for his four elements theory.

Water
Water is necessary for the survival of all living things. It is the liquid state of matter.

What Is Matter?

Everything around us is matter. If it takes up space, it is matter. This means that matter includes things that cannot be seen, such as air and gas, because they take up space. We use our senses to describe matter. Sight: is it shiny, dull, or colored? Smell and taste: is it sweet or bitter? Touch: is it soft, hard, dry, or wet? Matter is also described according to other qualities that it may have, such as bounciness, stretchiness, or magnetism.

Matter usually has one of three main properties. These are the three phases, or states, that matter can be in: gas, liquid, or solid. Scientists have also discovered some more unusual variations of these states, which are not so common on Earth. One of these states is plasma. This is usually a very hot gas that behaves differently from normal gas. The Sun and other stars are made of plasma. They are large balls of gas at extremely high temperatures.

That's Amazing!

Man-made plasma is in fluorescent lamps. Plasma also occurs in nature. For example, the aurora borealis, also known as the Northern Lights, is created by plasma from the Sun.

Solid

A solid is any form of matter that keeps its shape. Its volume does not change. It is also very difficult to compress.

Gas

A gas takes the shape of the container it is in. It flows easily and can be compressed. The density of a gas can vary.

Liquid

A liquid takes the shape of the container that holds it. It pours and flows easily, but is difficult to compress.

Solid, liquid, or gas?
All the objects in and around
this room are made of matter
in its different states: solid,
liquid, and gas.

Solid	Liquid	Gas
bed	boy (mostly water)	air
books	drink in bottle	air in bicycle tires
kite	"lava" in desk lamp	boy (contains some gas)
lamp	water in wall radiator	
mountain		
windows		

Which is which?
Some of the objects in and around the room above are listed (above)
according to which state of matter they are. Can you list any more?

Raindrops

When clouds become too heavy with water vapor, the water falls and turns into rain or snow, depending on the temperature. Raindrops can fall at speeds of up to 22 miles (35 km) per hour.

Raindrops hit the ground.

On the surface

A water strider's legs are covered with short hairs that trap tiny air bubbles. This allows the water strider to skate across the surface of water at about 3 feet (90 cm) per second.

Water strider

States of Water

W ater is the substance on Earth that is most commonly seen in all three main states of matter. When water is in solid form, we call it ice. When it is in a gas form, we usually call it steam, and when it is in liquid form, it is water. There are other names we have for water—for example, clouds, dew, and slush—which we use when the water is changing from one state to another. In Iceland, where ice is common, they have 45 different words for ice in its various stages.

It is possible to find water as a gas almost everywhere on Earth. However, water does not stay in its gaseous state for long because it cools as it rises in the atmosphere. And when it cools, it turns back into its liquid form, water droplets. In your kitchen you will find water in all its states: ice cubes in the freezer, water out of the faucet, and bubbles of water gas from the pot boiling on the stove.

Water and Earth

Water covers about two thirds of Earth's surface. Ice, which is the solid state of water, covers more than 10 percent of Earth's landmass.

Earth from space

Pack ice

Frozen seawater breaks away from land and floats on the currents and tides. When winds and storms drive it together in a large mass, it forms pack ice.

Opening through pack ice

That's Amazing!
The tallest iceberg ever measured reached 550 feet (168 m) high above the ocean. That is about the height of a 50-story building. It was in the North Atlantic Ocean.

Iceberg
An iceberg is freshwater turned to ice. About 90 percent of the volume of an iceberg is underwater.

Steam
Look just above the spout of a boiling kettle and you will find water in its gaseous form. But it is invisible. Then as the water gas cools, it turns into steam, which is tiny droplets of water.

Water gas and steam

Clouds
Clouds are made of millions of tiny water droplets or ice crystals that are about 1,000 times smaller than a raindrop. They are so light, they can float in the air.

Cumulus clouds

A Closer Look

A Greek scholar called Democritus believed that if objects were broken up into smaller and smaller pieces, eventually, you would have a piece of matter that could not be made any smaller. Although this theory was ignored for 2,000 years, we now know that matter is made from tiny particles called atoms. They cannot be seen even with the most powerful microscope. This page you are reading is probably about 1 million atoms thick.

There are only 98 different types of atoms that occur naturally. These different atoms make all the millions of different materials in the universe. Like the 26 letters of the English alphabet, which join together in different combinations to make millions of words, the different atom types join in different combinations to form molecules. All the different materials that we know of are made from combinations of atoms and molecules.

That's Amazing!

At sea level, water boils and changes into a gas at 212°F (100°C). At lower air pressure on top of Mount Everest, water boils at the lower temperature of around 156°F (69°C).

Smells fill the house

The tiny gas particles that are cooking smells leave the pots on the stove, bounce farther and farther apart, and gradually spread throughout a house.

Kitchen

Dining Room

Bedroom

Water molecules
One atom of oxygen combined with two atoms of hydrogen make one molecule of water. The tiny water molecules do not grip each other tightly, which gives water its liquid property.

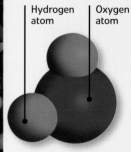

Hydrogen atom   Oxygen atom

Change of state
Matter may change state when its temperature is changed. The pressure surrounding matter will also affect its state.

Ice
Ice is water that has been cooled. The water molecules are packed close together and are difficult to break apart. Ice will keep its shape without a container.

Water
As ice is heated, the water molecules get excited and bounce farther apart. In this state they slide by each other. They need a container to keep them together or they will flow all over the floor.

Steam and water vapor
As water is heated, bubbles of gas form, called water vapor. When hot enough, gas molecules bounce even farther apart and leave the container. Steam above boiling water is tiny droplets of water in the vapor.

Changing Matter

Every day, changes in temperature cause changes in matter. These are often temporary changes. For example, clouds soon become water again as rain. Pressure changes are perhaps less obvious and less familiar. However, coal forms by pressure on vegetation left at the bottom of a swamp millions of years ago. Over time, under the pressure of layers of rock, the loosely packed molecules of vegetation were transformed into tightly packed molecules of solid coal.

Matter also changes as the result of a chemical reaction. For example, chemicals are added to crude oil to make plastics, and chemicals are also used to make nylon and polyester.

Temporary change

Matter has a temporary change of state when the outside influence, such as temperature, that changed it is removed and it returns to its original state.

Molten steel
Steel ingots heated to a high temperature turn the solid steel into a liquid.

Molded to shape
The molten steel is poured into a mold, then it cools to form solid steel rods.

Permanent change

Matter changes its state permanently when the external influence that changed it is removed but it does not go back to its original state.

Steel pipes
If steel pipes are exposed to air and water, the steel reacts chemically and changes.

Rusty pipes
The steel oxidizes, or rusts, making a different substance. It cannot be changed back into steel.

EXPERIMENT

If you follow the instructions carefully, you will observe that a chemical reaction can change matter. Here, a liquid mixed with a solid produces a gas. You will also see that the gas takes up more space than both the liquid and the solid.

You will need:
- A balloon
- A small funnel
- A spoon
- A plastic bottle
- Baking soda
- Vinegar

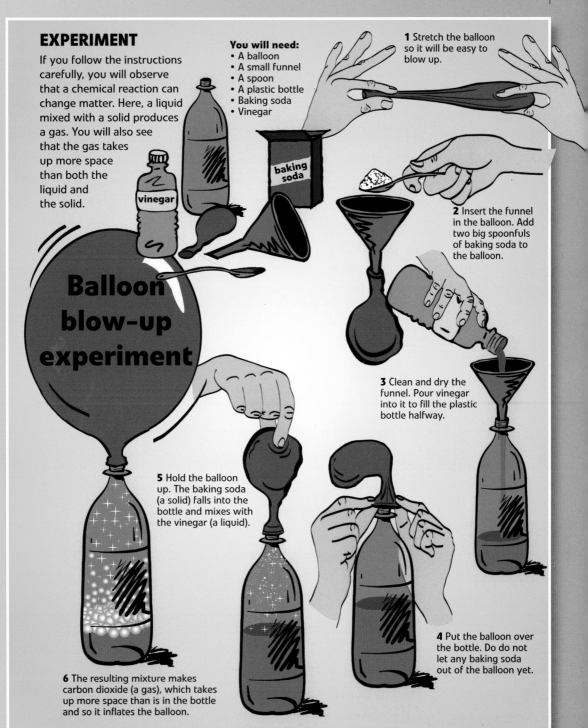

baking soda

vinegar

Balloon blow-up experiment

1 Stretch the balloon so it will be easy to blow up.

2 Insert the funnel in the balloon. Add two big spoonfuls of baking soda to the balloon.

3 Clean and dry the funnel. Pour vinegar into it to fill the plastic bottle halfway.

5 Hold the balloon up. The baking soda (a solid) falls into the bottle and mixes with the vinegar (a liquid).

4 Put the balloon over the bottle. Do do not let any baking soda out of the balloon yet.

6 The resulting mixture makes carbon dioxide (a gas), which takes up more space than is in the bottle and so it inflates the balloon.

Wacky, Weird, and Wonderful

Sometimes matter does not behave the way you would expect it to. Most liquids, when cooled and turned into a solid, will sink. But ice floats. This is because when water freezes, the water molecules spread out as they link up, so there are fewer molecules in a block of ice than in the same volume of water. Ice is therefore lighter than water, so it floats. During World War II, scientists used the floating property of ice to build an aircraft carrier out of pykrete, a mixture of 86 percent ice and 14 percent wood pulp. This top-secret project, called Operation Habakkuk, was eventually shelved in December 1943 after a great deal of research.

Scientists have created other strange materials for special purposes, including materials that get thicker instead of thinner when stretched, fluids that are magnetic, and fluids that get harder when you hit them.

Mercury
The only common metal that is liquid at room temperature, mercury was widely used in thermometers but it is very poisonous.

Dry ice
This is frozen carbon dioxide. When it thaws, it changes from a solid to a gas without first becoming a liquid.

Diamond
The hardest natural material known to humans was formed millions of years ago deep underground from pure carbon atoms.

Spider web
Spider's silk is stronger than high-grade steel and as strong as Kevlar, the material used in bulletproof vests. It is also light.

WACKY MATTER EXPERIMENT

A dilatant is a liquid that gets harder when it is squeezed. You can make a dilatant by mixing cornstarch with water. Collect what you need for this experiment. Put cornstarch in a bowl and add a little water at a time, stirring constantly. Do not add too much water. The liquid needs to be like a very thick pancake mix. Stick your hand in the liquid and see what it feels like. It will run through your fingers like a liquid, but if you hit the mixture with your hand, it feels more like a solid.

What you need:
- 2 cups cornstarch
- About 1 cup water
- A spoon
- A mixing bowl

Now it is a liquid
Cornstarch mixed with water makes a suspension because the large cornstarch molecules do not combine with the small water molecules. When you dip your hand in, it feels like a liquid.

Now it is a solid
Now hit the surface of the liquid with the back of your hand or the back of a spoon. When the molecules compress, they line up so the liquid behaves more like a solid. A dilatant does not splash.

Discovery and splitting

Although Ernest Rutherford is credited with the theory of the atomic model, he had fine colleagues to help him and to carry on his work. Ernest Walton and John Cockcroft, members of Rutherford's team, later went on to win the Nobel Prize in Physics in 1951 for their pioneering work in changing the nucleus of an atom by bombarding it with atomic particles. Their work paved the way for scientists to develop nuclear energy and the infamous atomic bomb.

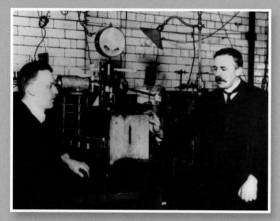

Hans Geiger with Ernest Rutherford
Hans Geiger (left) helped Rutherford formulate many of his ideas about atomic structure. He also co-invented the Geiger counter, used for measuring radioactivity.

John Cockcroft
In 1932, Cockcroft and Ernest Walton built a high-voltage machine to shoot protons down an 8-foot (2.4-m) tube. With this, they split the nucleus of a targeted lithium atom.

Atom structure

Scientists think that each atom consists of particles: protons and neutrons jiggle within the nucleus; quarks jiggle inside them; while electrons move constantly around the nucleus. But 99.999999 percent of an atom's volume is empty space.

Nucleus
This is the atom's center, its heaviest part, and it is composed of neutrons and protons. The atom shown here contains two neutrons and two protons.

Quark
Quarks (some green, some lilac) combine to form protons and neutrons. Quarks come in different flavors with odd names such as up, down, top, bottom, charm, and strange.

Splitting the Atom

Electron
Members of the lepton family of particles, electrons are tiny, negatively charged particles that move around an atom's nucleus.

Until the early 1900s, scientists believed that the atom was the smallest particle in the universe and that all matter was made from atoms. At the time, Ernest Rutherford was researching radioactivity in uranium. From his experiments, he theorized that an atom was made up of a nucleus with electrons circling around it. His team of scientists at Cavendish Laboratory, at Cambridge University in England, later went on to prove that an atom could be split into these different parts.

Rutherford's pioneering research led the way for today's scientists, who continue to find new ways to split the atom into even smaller parts. In support of Democritus's theory, their goal is to understand the ultimate underlying structure of all matter.

That's Amazing!
Imagine if an atom were the size of a football field. Its nucleus would be as big as a piece of popcorn.

Neutrons and protons
Neutrons (large blue spheres) in the atom's nucleus have no electrical charge. Protons (large orange spheres) have a positive charge.

Nuclear power station
Splitting atoms generates a huge amount of heat, used to turn water into steam in nuclear power stations. The steam drives turbines, which generate electricity.

The Big Bang

Where did all the matter come from? Scientists believe that about 13.7 billion years ago, all the material to make the entire universe we can see today was smaller than a pinhead. It was hotter and more dense than anything imaginable. Then something made this tiny point start expanding. The universe was born and has continued to expand at a fantastic rate.

13.7 billion years ago
The cosmos grows from the size of an atom to a basketball in a fraction of a trillionth of a second. Particles and antiparticles form and then destroy each other. After three minutes, some of the remaining protons and neutrons join, creating helium nuclei.

380,000 years later
The cosmos has cooled to 18,000°F (10,000°C). Protons and neutrons start to capture electrons, so atoms form. The universe is filled with clouds of helium and hydrogen atoms.

1 billion years later
The cosmos is a cold place now, with a temperature of about −328°F (−200°C). Gravity causes clouds of gases to clump together and the first galaxies and stars form.

BALLOON EXPERIMENT

Put as many small dots on a deflated balloon as you can. Blow up the balloon. The dots (galaxies) get farther apart as the balloon (universe) expands.

Deflated   Inflated

Big Bang time line

The raw ingredient of the universe is energy. As the universe cooled, tiny particles formed and eventually clumped together to make the building blocks of the universe as it is now.

Stars and galaxies evolve
Generations of massive stars are born and die. Galaxies gradually take on the appearance they have today.

Solar System is born
About 9 billion years after the Big Bang, our Solar System appears.

Today
Some stars are dying, sending heavy elements into space. Galaxies cluster together under the force of gravity. New stars are being born from the remains of dead stars.

Matter and Antimatter

S cientists now know that for every particle there is an antiparticle. The first scientist to predict this was Paul Dirac. He won the Nobel Prize in Physics in 1933 for this theory after scientists proved it by creating a positron, which is the antiparticle of an electron.

The Big Bang theory tells us that it takes a great deal of energy to make matter. When matter meets its corresponding antimatter, both the matter and antimatter disappear, but all the energy that went into making them both is released. Scientists call this process annihilation. When annihilation occurs and all that energy is released, the more matter and antimatter there is, the bigger the bang.

Matter meets antimatter
Matter and antimatter meet and annihilate each other. Luckily, only tiny quantities of antimatter exist on Earth.

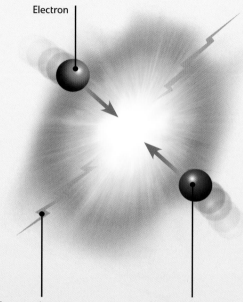

Electron

Gamma photons

Antielectron

PET SCANNER

Positron emission tomography (PET) scanners examine the internal workings of the human body in more detail than X-rays can. A patient is injected with a special fluid that emits positrons, created in a nuclear laboratory. The positrons quickly encounter electrons in the body and annihilate them in a flash of gamma rays. These escape from the patient's body to be detected by the PET scanner.

Scanner in action
A patient enters the machine. The gamma radiation is too weak to pose a serious risk to body tissue.

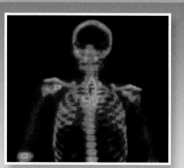

Image from scanner
A computer builds up 3-D images of the annihilation sites, helping doctors diagnose internal problems.

Lightning
A telescope in space unexpectedly found gamma rays, which looked like those from collisions of matter and antimatter. These rays were coming from Earth's atmosphere during severe lightning storms.

Where is all the antimatter?
Only tiny amounts of antimatter have been detected on Earth and in our galaxy. The universe produced in the Big Bang is dominated by matter, for reasons we do not fully understand.

Particle Accelerators

S cientists use particle accelerators to study atomic nuclei. Scientists shoot different particles into a tube, and then accelerate them to speeds close to the speed of light. At this point, they smash the particles into each other or into a stationary object and record what happens. By looking at new particles that are produced, and measuring their energy, scientists learn about the basic structure of matter and how different types of particles are related.

The largest particle accelerator in the world is called the Large Hadron Collider (LHC), which is run by the European Organization for Nuclear Research (CERN). The accelerator tube is a tunnel deep underground, and it is so big that it crosses the border between France and Switzerland.

1 Meyrin site
These buildings contain all the powerful computer equipment used to process the data from experiments.

4 Access tunnel
Equipment is lowered down one of the access tunnels during the construction of the LHC.

Large Hadron Collider

The tunnel that houses the LHC is 17 miles (27 km) around and up to 574 feet (175 m) underground. Scientists expect that when it is fully operational, it will give more clues about the origin of matter.

Switzerland

France

Border between Switzerland and France

KEY

Electron
Positron

5 Cutaway of the collider
The superconducting magnets and outer cooling layer surround the particle accelerator tubes.

2 Collision event
This is what scientists see when there is a collision event inside the LHC. The lines are the paths the particles took after colliding at high speed.

3 Prévessin site
This is the largest site for doing experiments at CERN. It has its own equipment for nuclear experiments.

Famous Scientists

Our knowledge of matter has grown rapidly over the last 200 years thanks to the contributions of many scientists working in the areas of physics, chemistry, mathematics, and astronomy. Progress has often occurred when scientists explored beyond their standard areas of expertise. Here are a few of the more notable researchers in the field of matter.

During the next 50 years, there will undoubtedly be many revelations in this area of research. Scientists will develop an even better understanding of the nature of everything that makes up the universe.

John Dalton (1766–1844)
Dalton discovered the law of heated gases expanding, proposed a modern atomic theory, and calculated the atomic weight of elements.

J. J. Thomson (1856–1940)
Thomson experimented with electricity traveling through gas and received the 1906 Nobel Prize in Physics for his work on electrons.

Ernest Rutherford (1871–1937)
A student of Thomson, Rutherford researched alpha ray scattering and developed the theory of what makes up an atom.

EINSTEIN'S THEORY

This explains the relationship between energy and mass in a famous formula, E=mc². This means energy (E) is equal to mass (m) multiplied by the speed of light (c) multiplied by itself (squared). A small amount of mass can be converted into a very large amount of energy.

Einstein's famous formula

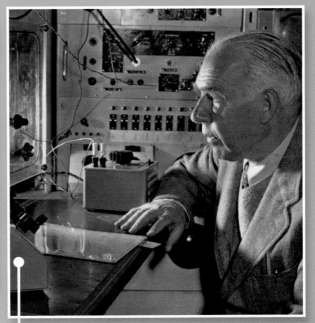

Albert Einstein (1879–1955)
Most famous for his theory of relativity, Einstein won the 1921 Nobel Prize in physics for his work in theoretical physics.

Niels Bohr (1885–1962)
This Danish physicist won the 1922 Nobel Prize in physics for his work on atoms. He promoted the peaceful use of atomic energy.

James Chadwick (1891–1974)
A colleague of Rutherford, Chadwick discovered the neutron, received the 1935 Nobel Prize, and worked on the atomic bomb.

Steven Chu (born 1948)
This US physicist won the 1997 Nobel Prize in physics for his research into the capturing of atoms using lasers.

Unsolved Mysteries

There are still many unsolved mysteries about matter and the forces that bind matter together. Existing evidence points to the fact that 96 percent of the universe is dark matter and dark energy, and yet scientists know almost nothing about them.

Closely related to this is the role of gravity in the universe. One of the many interesting facts is that time runs faster when the gravitational force is lower. Scientists have placed very accurate atomic clocks in satellites and compared them with similar clocks on Earth. Time runs faster on the satellite. This means that time must get slower as you get closer to the high gravity caused by a black hole in space.

Dark matter and dark energy
By observing the effect of gravity in the universe, scientists believe the universe is 4 percent visible matter, which we can see, 22 percent dark matter, and 74 percent dark energy, both of which we cannot see.

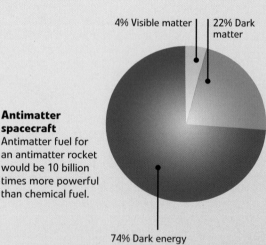

4% Visible matter | 22% Dark matter

74% Dark energy

Antimatter spacecraft
Antimatter fuel for an antimatter rocket would be 10 billion times more powerful than chemical fuel.

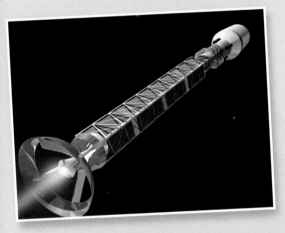

Viking lander on Mars
Two *Viking* landers on Mars did experiments for signs of life. The results were unclear.

Positron reaction motor
This illustration by NASA scientists uses antimatter to drive a rocket motor. But can they build it and operate it?

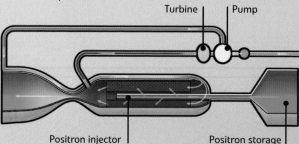

Turbine | Pump

Positron injector | Positron storage

Dark matter

NASA scientists believe this image shows dark matter and normal matter becoming separated as two clusters of galaxies collide. The blue areas are where most of the dark matter must be, but cannot be seen.

ULTRA DEEP FIELD

The Hubble Space Telescope is looking back into space to search for galaxies that may have existed shortly after the Big Bang. This image of a tiny section of sky, about .0016 square inches (1 sq mm) viewed at arm's length, is the deepest space image ever recorded. This tiny bit of sky contains about 10,000 galaxies.

Deep space

Glossary

antimatter
(AN-tee-mat-ur)
Matter made up of antiparticles rather than normal particles.

atom (AT-um)
A basic unit of matter.

cosmos (KOZ-mos)
The universe.

electron (ih-LEK-tron)
A tiny, low-mass particle that moves around the nucleus of an atom and carries a negative charge.

element (EL-luh-munt)
A chemical substance formed from one type of atom only.

galaxy (GAL-ik-see)
A massive group of stars, gas, and dust held together by gravity.

gamma rays
(GAM-uh RAYZ)
Very high-energy electromagnetic rays given off by a radioactive substance and in other high-energy processes.

gaseous (GA-shus)
Having the properties of a gas.

Geiger counter
(GY-gur KOWN-tur)
A device used for measuring radioactivity.

helium (HEE-lee-um)
The second-lightest element, seen on Earth as a gas that is lighter than air.

leptons (LEP-tonz)
A family of subatomic particles that includes electrons and positrons.

molecules
(MAH-lih-kyoolz)
A group of atoms joined together, forming the smallest unit of a chemical substance.

nucleus (NOO-klee-us)
The dense center of an atom.

particle accelerator
(PAR-tih-kul
ik-SEH-luh-rayt-ur)
A device used for smashing particles into each other at high speeds.

plasma (PLAZ-muh)
A highly conductive gas that responds strongly to electromagnetic forces.

protons (PROH-tonz)
Particles with a positive charge that, together with neutrons, make up the nucleus of all atoms.

quark (KWARK)
A subatomic particle that is a basic constituent of matter, especially protons and neutrons.

superconducting magnets
(SOO-per-kun-duk-ting MAG-nets)
Electromagnets built using superconducting wire kept at very cold temperatures.

suspension
(suh-SPENT-shun)
A substance whose particles are mixed with, but not dissolved in, a fluid.

universe (YOO-nih-vers)
The whole of space and everything that exists in it, such as stars, planets, and even energy.

Index

A
annihilation 22
antimatter 20, 22, 23, 28
antimatter spacecraft 28
atom splitting 18, 19
atoms 6, 12, 13, 16, 18, 19, 20, 26, 27
aurora borealis 8
Ayurveda 6

B
balloon blow-up experiment 15
balloon experiment 21
Big Bang theory 20, 21, 22, 29
black hole 28

C
cosmos 20

D
dark energy 28
dark matter 28, 29
Democritus 6, 12
diamond 16
dry ice 16

E
Einstein's theory 27
electrons 18, 19, 20, 22, 24, 26
elements 6, 7, 21, 27
Empedocles 6, 7

G
galaxies 20, 21, 23, 29
Geiger counter 18

H
Hubble Space Telescope 29

I
ice 10, 11, 12, 16
iceberg 11

L
Large Hadron Collider 24, 25
lepton 19

M
matter 6, 7, 8, 9, 10, 12, 14, 15, 16, 19, 20, 22, 23, 24, 26, 28, 29
mercury 16
molecules 12, 13, 14, 16, 17

N
neutron 18, 19, 20, 27
nuclear power 19
nucleus 18, 19

O
Operation Habakkuk 16

P
particle accelerators 24, 25
PET scanner 22
phases of matter 8

plasma 8
positron reactor motor 28
protons 18, 19, 20
pykrete 16

Q
quark 18

S
scientists 6, 16, 18, 19, 20, 22, 24, 25, 26, 27, 28, 29
spider webs 17
stars 8, 20, 21
state changes, permanent 14
state changes, temporary 14
states of matter 8, 9, 10
states of water 10, 11, 12, 13
steam 6, 10, 11, 13, 19
superconducting magnets 24

U
universe 6, 12, 19, 20, 21, 23, 26, 28

V
Viking lander 28

W
wacky matter 16, 17

Websites

Due to the changing nature of Internet links, PowerKids Press has developed an online list of websites related to the subject of this book. This site is updated regularly. Please use this link to access the list:

www.powerkidslinks.com/disc/matter/

AUG 1 2 1974

AUG 2 2 2014